VANGE

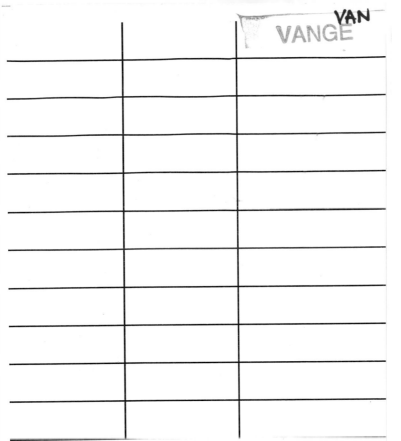

Please return this book on or before the date shown above. To renew go to www.essex.gov.uk/libraries, ring 0345 603 7628 or go to any Essex library.

Essex County Council

Ali and Annie's Guide to...

Coping with
Bullying

Claire Throp

raintree

a Capstone company — publishers for children

Raintree is an imprint of Capstone Global Library Limited, a company incorporated in England and Wales having its registered office at 264 Banbury Road, Oxford, OX2 7DY – Registered company number: 6695582

www.raintree.co.uk
myorders@raintree.co.uk

Edited by Clare Lewis and Helen Cox Cannons
Designed by Dynamo
Original illustrations © Capstone Global Library Limited 2019
Picture research by Dynamo
Production by Tori Abraham
Originated by Capstone Global Library Limited
Printed and bound in India

ISBN 978 1 4747 7304 1
22 21 20 19
10 9 8 7 6 5 4 3 2 1

British Library Cataloguing in Publication Data
A full catalogue record for this book is available from the British Library.

Acknowledgements
We would like to thank the following for permission to reproduce photographs:
Getty Images: Cultura/Phil Boorman, 28, DigitalVision/Chris Whitehead, 9, 26-27, DigitalVision/Richard Lewisohn, 5 Top Right, E+/andresr, 11, E+/FatCamera, 23, E+/SolStock, 24, E+/Steve Debenport, 21, E+/sturti, 19, Image Source, 10, iStock/bowdenimages, Cover, 1, iStock/ClarkandCompany, 16, iStock/LightFieldStudios, 8, iStock/monkeybusinessimages, 13, 17, iStock/patat, 14, iStock/Wavebreakmedia, 27, iStock/YakobchukOlena, 20, Photographer's Choice RF/Roger Spooner, 25, Tetra Images, 18, The Image Bank/Peter Dazeley, 15, VisitBritain/Rod Edwards, 22, Westend61, 4-5, 6-7, 7 Bottom Right, 12.

We would like to thank Charlotte Mitchell for her invaluable help with the preparation of this book.

Contents

I'm Ali! Look out for our helpful tips throughout the book.

Hi! I'm Annie and this is my dog, Charlie.

Some words are shown in bold, **like this**. You can find out what they mean by looking in the glossary.

What is bullying?

Bullying is when someone focuses on something about a person and is unkind about it. It can be **physical** or **verbal**. It is done on purpose. It can sometimes go on for a long period of time. It can make the bullied person's life miserable.

▲ Bullying can make you feel very alone.

Bullying can happen anywhere. It can take place at school. It can happen at home or at other people's homes. It can happen **online**. Bullying can also happen in public places like parks or sports clubs.

Bullying can happen to anyone

Bullying can affect anyone. Bullies often pick on people they see as "different". It could be their skin colour, religion or even accent. Sometimes bullying can happen for no particular reason. Whatever the reason, though, bullying is always wrong.

▶ Bullying can make you feel very sad. But it will not last forever.

TIP

Remember that being bullied is not something to be ashamed of. It is not your fault.

Who bullies?

People become bullies for different reasons. Some bullies have been or are being bullied themselves. They bully others to try to feel they have some control over their lives.

▲ Sometimes bullies are people who feel angry about things that are happening to them.

▲ Whatever the reason for bullying, it is never right.

Some people become bullies because they think it will impress their friends. Others bully because they are **jealous** of the person they are bullying. That person may have something the bully wants, or may be more clever or talented than the bully.

Types of bullying

There are many different types of bullying. A bully may push, kick or hit the person they are bullying. They may say cruel things or not include someone in a group any more.

It is much easier to pick on people if you are part of a group. Bullies can find themselves being unkind just to fit in with their friends.

◀ You may feel lonely, but there is always someone who can help you.

TIP

Remember, no one deserves to be bullied. You don't need to go through it alone.

Physical bullying

Physical bullying is when someone hurts or injures someone else on purpose. Pushing someone over or hitting them can make the bully feel powerful. It makes the person being bullied feel powerless. That makes the bully feel even stronger.

TIP

If you are being physically bullied, try not to fight back. You may end up getting badly hurt or hurting the bully.

Verbal bullying

Bullying is not always obvious. Adults may not always see that it's happening. When people call you hurtful names over and over again, it is verbal bullying. Talking about you behind your back or spreading rumours is also verbal bullying.

Finding out someone has spread nasty rumours about you can be very upsetting.

▲ Non-violent bullying can be just as hurtful as physical bullying.

Emotional bullying

Emotional bullying is another type of bullying. The bully may try to force you out of your group of friends, **threaten** you, try to embarrass you or **mock** you.

Cyberbullying

Cyberbullying is any kind of bullying that happens online. You may be playing an online game and another player begins to say nasty things. They may gang up on you with other players.

Hurtful text messages or social media comments are also cyberbullying.

This type of bullying is just like other types – it is always wrong. Take a break from your phone or the computer for a while. The best way to deal with cyberbullying is to ignore the bully and tell an adult you trust what has happened.

TIP

Remember to always respect other people online. Try to think about the effect your comments might have on them.

Talking to someone

You might think it's best not to tell on bullies in case they hurt you more. You might think an adult won't believe you or can't help anyway. But you should always tell an adult you trust. Whether it's your parents, carers or a teacher, they will be able to help you.

Find an adult who will listen to you.

Your actions may also help other children who are being bullied by the same person. Those children might be too scared to speak up.

▼ Parents and teachers may be able to work together to help you.

TIP

It can also help to talk to your friends. Their **support** will help you to get through the difficult times.

Expressing your feelings

Writing or drawing can help you to **express** your **emotions**. You could keep a diary. It is normal to feel angry about being bullied. Writing how you feel each day may make you feel better.

Writing or drawing about your feelings can help you work out how you feel.

You could write a letter to the person who is bullying you. You don't need to send the letter. Just writing down how their bullying makes you feel can help. When you have written your letter, you could show it to a trusted adult. It might help them to understand how you feel.

Friends can give you lots of support.

Trying something new

TIP

Try to do things you enjoy with people you like who also like you back. You will feel much happier about life.

Try a new activity! Joining a sports club, for example, could be a way to make new friends. This may help you to feel more **confident**. And you will get fitter and healthier at the same time!

Taking up a new hobby, such as painting, can help you too. It will give you something more **positive** to focus on.

11

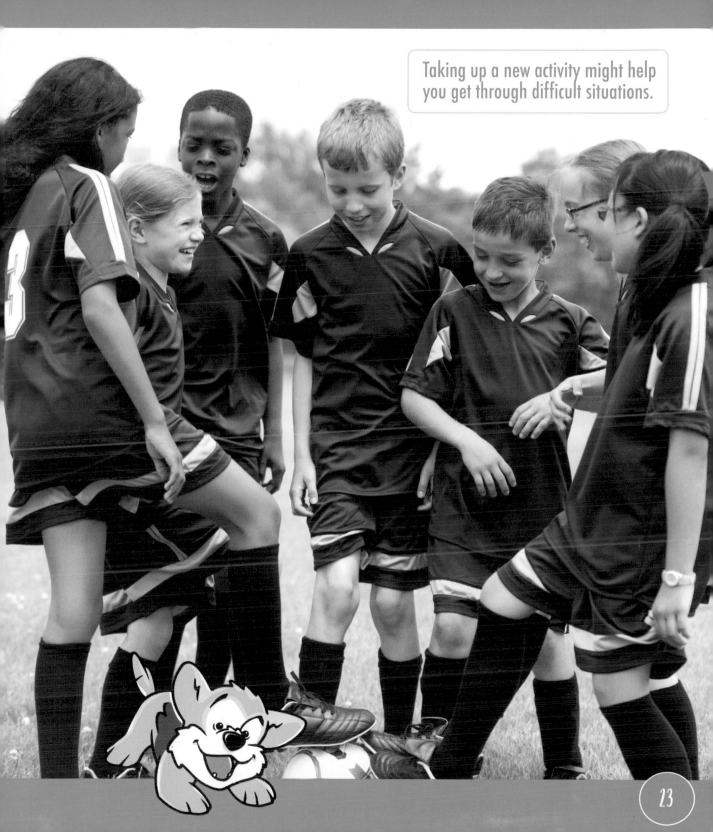

Taking up a new activity might help you get through difficult situations.

Do you bully?

Have you ever bullied someone? Before you bully again, stop and think. Imagine how the person being bullied is feeling. If you have been bullied, you will know how hurtful it is.

▲ Online bullying causes just as much pain as physical bullying.

Why do you bully? You may have started bullying in order to feel in control of your life. Try to sort out any problems you may have by talking to someone. It will help you to feel better about yourself. Then you will no longer feel the need to bully others.

Is someone being bullied?

If you think someone you know is being bullied, try to help them. If the person being bullied is your friend, talk to them. Try to find out what the problem is. Encourage them to tell an adult. Make sure you give them as much support as you can.

▶ Don't support a bully. If you see someone being bullied, tell an adult about it.

Even if the person being bullied isn't a friend of yours, be friendly towards them. Again, get them to talk to someone they trust. Don't try to fight the bullies yourselves.

▲ It is important to listen to friends if they are being bullied.

Dealing with bullying

Bullying is always wrong! Never believe that it is just part of growing up. Never believe that it's your fault. It isn't. Bullying is horrible and makes you feel miserable. Talking to a trusted adult will help. Spending time with friends and family who love you will help too!

Ali and Annie's advice

- ★ Try not to fight back against a physical bully. Tell an adult about it instead.

- ★ Ignore the cyberbullies online.

- ★ Tell an adult if you are being bullied.

- ★ Don't blame yourself – it's not your fault that you are being bullied.

- ★ Write a diary every day or draw a picture to express your feelings.

- ★ Make time to be with your friends.

- ★ Take up a new activity. It will help you to become confident again.

- ★ Be yourself!

Glossary

confident being sure of yourself or feeling good about yourself

cyberbullying bullying that happens online or on a mobile phone, such as by text message, on social media or through comments on live online games

emotions feelings

express say or show how you feel about yourself to other people

jealous wanting something that someone else has, such as lots of friends, a new bike or to be really good at singing or sport

mock tease or laugh at someone, often for being different

online on the internet

physical to do with the body, not the mind

positive hopeful

support help someone by being there for them when they are going through a difficult time

threaten tell someone you're going to do something horrible to them, in order to make them feel scared or worried

verbal to do with words and what people say

Find out more

Books

Dealing with Bullying, Jane Lacey (Franklin Watts, 2017)

Questions and Feelings About Bullying, Louise Spilsbury (Franklin Watts, 2018)

Say No to Bullying, Louise Spilsbury (Wayland, 2014)

Websites

www.anti-bullyingalliance.org.uk/tools-information/if-youre-being-bullied/i-am-being-bullied

This website has lots of great tips to help you deal with bullies.

www.bullying.co.uk

This website has all kinds of advice to help fight against bullying.

www.childline.org.uk/info-advice/bullying-abuse-safety

If you want help about anything, from bullying to exams, visit the Childline website.